Unlaunch'd Voices

An Evening with Walt Whitman

A Play by
Michael Z. Keamy

To PAT,

Best Wishes!

Stephs Collini

as

Walt Whitman

Acknowledgement

Special thanks to Stephen Collins who inspired and first performed this play.

A Note on the Text

Walt Whitman's poetry appears in *italics*.

A Note on Slides

The use of period slides assist in creating a visual, historical sense of place and at times reveal the poet's subconscious. Images were gathered from Matthew Brady's extensive collection of Civil War photos, anatomical slides from Grey's Anatomy as well as other readily available images from historical and Whitman family archives.

Act One

(May 31, 1889, Walt Whitman's bedroom/study. The space is very cluttered; piles of books, manuscripts, newspapers, etc. cover the desk, floor and chairs. There is a window upstage center and a doorway stage right leading to a hallway. Walt Whitman is seventy. He wears an overcoat and hat. A recent stroke leaves him dependent on a wheelchair and cane.)

(In dark)   Horace!

(Lights up. Walt calls out of window) Horace!

I've searched everywhere, I can't find it! Hold on...
(Calling offstage) Mrs. Davis, did you see Horace's notebook while you were cleaning?
(Listens) Near the pile of books? *Which* pile of books?

(Walt searches downstage.)

(Noticing audience) Well, hello! *Howdy'do?* Excuse me for a moment, please...I... *(Back to window)* Horace, I can't find it! No, don't come back up, It will turn up somewhere. I'll give it to you tonight. You'll bring the carriage 'round at eight o'clock? Fine, fine. Yes, I'll be here. If a party is being held for Walt Whitman then Walt Whitman himself had best show up!

(To audience) Howdy'do! Forgive the confusion...excuse the mess. I'm glad you found a spot to sit down. Mrs. Davis, my housekeeper, calls this room "utterly indecent, disorder added to disorder. Not a fit place for a man or his visitors!"

Well…I reminded her of what a critic once said about my book *Leaves of Grass*- "It is a confused book. The author gets mixed up at the start and is never put to order again." '*That* explains this room, Mrs. Davis,' I said.

Nevertheless, when she heard you were coming she took it upon herself to "tidy things up."

(A whisper) She has arranged everything so I don't know where a damn thing is! Bless her; I know her heart is in the right place. As is Horace's heart…

Horace and his notebook! Oh, Horace is my friend and neighbor. He visits every day now, you know, records our conversations, writes everything I say down in his little notebook. Oh, I don't mind. In fact I want him to as long as he writes about me honest, doesn't prettify me – I told him just be sure to include all the hells and damns!

But how are you? Howdy' do? *How-Dy-Do.* Ain't that a good word? It has phonetic significance…a truly American greeting. It rolls off the tongue more readily than *"Good evening"* don't you think?

Myself?

Well…

3

The doctor says that from a medical point of view I'm getting along alright. But from my point of view I'm in a pretty boggy condition indeed. But, if the doctor feels alright about it I don't suppose it matters what I feel. I like to see the doctor comfortable anyway.

I *can* still write, read, work. I can laugh, cry, be myself in most ways. I suppose I shouldn't kick because I can't climb mountains. But *seventy?* Tonight there is a celebration in honor of my seventieth year.

Seventy years…

I suppose it's fitting then that you're here and that you want to know about me and the Leaves. My *Leaves of Grass*.

I've had lots of visitors lately. Do you know Oscar Wilde? He was here… a fine, large handsome youngster. And smart. He had the good sense to take a liking to me. But I don't agree with his "art for art's sake" notions. Like literature for literature's sake. Writing created on such a principle removes us from humanity. It is only from humanity that the light can come.

I never wanted to be a witness for saviors or exceptional men. I wanted *Leaves of Grass* to be read by the average man, the common man, like yourself.

(Walt retrieves and reads from a copy of Leaves of Grass) "The proof of a poet is that his country absorbs him as affectionately as he has absorbed it." My words. The task I set for myself right at the start. Now as I sit here gossiping in the candlelight of old age, I and my book, casting a 'backward glance o'er travel'd roads'...I must admit I have not been embraced. Not by those that mean the most to me.

I know from a business and worldly point of view, *Leaves of Grass* has proved to be worse than a failure. I cannot separate the book from myself. I have thrown my life into it. It was always the book, giving it all, all. But the people... I've had no way of reaching them. I needed to reach the people but...I...
(Aware of audience) I am getting to be a sort of monologuer. It's a disease that grows on a man who has no legs to walk on.

You know, when I was younger I wanted to be an orator. I knew I had something to say and was afraid I'd get no chance to say it through books. I was full of designs for things that were never executed- lectures, songs, *plays*, God help me!

It took me some time to get down -or *up* -to my proper measure. I was writing for years with no particular direction. The words seemed disconnected from myself, my true self... my soul. Then in my mid-thirties it occurred to me that America, like myself, had yet to find its own voice, its own poetry. It was this – the desire to be America's poet that really got me started.

I took to the open air, to nature and wrote, wrote, wrote...the words came spilling out.

I had an experience at that time. A mystical experience you might call it. One early summer morning I walked far out into a field. I was alone and quiet was all around me... I lay down on the damp earth... I felt the morning sun on my face. I asked my soul to-

(As Walt recites his poem, he slowly stands, sheds his coat,
unbuttons his shirt and rolls up his sleeves, transforming
into his younger, vibrant, healthy self.)

Loaf with me on the grass, loose the stop from your throat,
Not words, not music or rhyme I want, not custom or
lecture, not even the best,
Only the lull I like, the hum of your valv'd voice.
I mind how once we lay such a transparent summer
morning,
how you settled your head athwart my hips and gently
turn'd over
upon me,
And parted the shirt from my bosom-bone, and plunged
your
tongue to my bare-stript heart,
And reach'd till you felt my beard, and reach'd till you held
my feet.

Swiftly arose and spread around me the peace and
knowledge that
pass all the argument of the earth,
And I know that the hand of God is the promise of my own,

and I know that the spirit of God is the brother of my own,
and that all the men ever born are also my brothers, and
the women my sisters and lovers,
And that a kelson of the creation is love,
And limitless are leaves stiff or drooping in the fields,
And brown ants in the little wells beneath them,
And mossy scabs of the worm fence, heap'd stones, elder,
mullein and poke-weed.

(Taking notice of his new 'self') I cannot be awake, for
nothing looks to me as it did before,
or else I am awake for the first time, and all before has been
a mean sleep!

I created a character, like me yet unlike me, an extension of
myself – the way I longed to be perceived. This Walt
Whitman was one of my changes of garments.

Walt Whitman, a kosmos, of Manhattan the son, turbulent,
fleshy, sensual, eating, drinking and breeding,
No sentimentalist, no stander above men and women or
apart from them,
No more modest that immodest.

Unscrew the locks from the doors!
Unscrew the doors themselves from their jambs!

The poems flowed from me-

(Walt picks poems to read from desk, floor, boxes, etc as if in a random order.)

I celebrate myself and sing myself,
And what I assume you shall assume,
For every atom belonging to me as good belongs to you.

I loaf and invite my soul,
I lean and loaf observing a spear of summer grass.
My tongue, every atom of my blood, form'd from this soil,
This air,
Born here of parents born here from parents the same, and
Their parents the same,
I, now 37 years old – in perfect health begin,
Hoping to cease not 'til death.

(A new poem. Walt's cane becomes a walking stick.)

Afoot and lighthearted I take to the open road,
Healthy, free, the world before me,
The long brown path before me leading wherever I choose.
Henceforth I ask not good fortune, I myself am good
fortune, henceforth I whimper no more, postpone no more,
need nothing,
Done with indoor complaints, libraries, querulous
criticisms,
Strong and content I travel the open road.

(New poem)

Have you reckon'd a thousand acres much? Have you
reckon'd the earth much?
Have you practic'd so long to learn to read?

Have you felt so proud to get at the meaning of poems?
Stop this day and night with me and you shall possess the
origin of all poems,
You shall possess the good of the earth and sun, (there are
millions of suns left.)
You shall no longer take things at second or third hand, nor
look through the eyes of the dead, nor feed on the specters
of books,

You shall not look through my eyes either, not take things from me,
You shall listen to all sides and filter them from yourself.

(New poem)

Take my leaves America, take them South and take them North,
Make welcome for them everywhere for they are your own offspring.
Surround them east and west for they would surround you,
and you precedents, connect lovingly with them, for they connect lovingly with you.
I conn'd old times; I sat studying at the feet of the great masters, now if eligible O that the great masters might return and study me.

Dead poets, philosophers, priests,
Martyrs, artists, inventors, governments long since,
Language shapers on other shores, nations once powerful, now reduced, withdrawn or desolate,
I dare not proceed till I respectfully credit what you have wafted hither.

11

I have perused it, own it as admirable,
(moving a while among it)
Think nothing can ever be greater, nothing can ever
deserve
More than it deserves,
Regarding it all intently a long while, then dismissing it,
I stand in my own place with my own day here.
My own day...

Having my own day wasn't easy. From the start, I was surrounded by opposition and advice. Even concerning the title, *Leaves of Grass*. "There are no *leaves* of grass, Walt, those are *your* words. There are spears of grass, spears, spears" But *spears* of grass would not have been the same to me. Etymologically, leaves *is* correct.

So I stuck with it. *Leaves*.

I never write a word that somebody don't object to. The thing that one likes, another don't. It is God bless you for this and Goddamn you for that. I used to think God was everywhere. I was wrong. The adviser is everywhere! Well, take *my* advice. Never take advice.

I published the poems myself, set the type myself, paid the printing costs myself.

Soon reviews appeared praising *Leaves of Grass*…written, anonymously, by me.

And then there were the other reviews …

(Reading from newspaper clippings)

"Who is this arrogant young man who proclaims himself the poet of time and who roots like a pig among the rotten garbage of licentious thoughts?"

(New clipping)

"This *Leaves of Grass* is a heterogeneous mass of bombast, egotism, vulgarity and nonsense."

(New clipping)

"It is impossible to imagine how any man's fancy could have conceived such a mass of stupid filth unless he were possessed of the soul of a sentimental donkey that has died of disappointed love."

(Pause) I don't know if you ever realized what it means to be a horror in the sight of the people about you.

I also sent first copies of *Leaves of Grass* to various esteemed men of letters. I got little response.

But one – *one* of those responses was great. So great I keep it here, close to me in my chest pocket. May I read it to you?

(Slide of Emerson)
(Walt reads letter.)
Dear Sir,

I am not blind to the worth of the wonderful gift of *Leaves of Grass.* I find it the most extraordinary piece of wit and wisdom that America has yet contributed. I am very happy in reading it, as great power makes us happy...

I give you joy of your free and brave thought. I have great joy in it. I find incomparable things said incomparably well, as they must be. I find the courage of treatment, which so delights me, and which large perception only can inspire. I greet you at the beginning of a great career, which yet must have had a long foreground somewhere for such a start. I rubbed my eyes a little to see if this sunbeam were no illusion; but the solid sense of the book is a sober certainty. It has the best merits, namely, of fortifying and encouraging.

I wish to see my benefactor, and have felt much like striking my tasks, and visiting New York to pay you my respects.

Ralph Waldo Emerson

(Slide out)
Oh! This letter electrified me! This glorious letter! It inspired me to continue writing with "free and brave thought."

And so I did.
It's funny. In retrospect it's funny that this man who motivated me so, this idol, this Emerson, was later, too, to advize.

Have you been to Boston?
I have several times, once to visit with Emerson…strange old Boston, with its zigzag streets and multitudinous angles. Crush up a piece of letter paper in your hand, throw it down, stamp it flat, and there you have a map of old Boston.

I've spent a good deal of time walking on Boston Common. I know all the big trees along Tremont and Beacon Streets. I have come to a sociable, silent understanding with most of them. Between these elms I walked for two hours one bright, sharp February with Emerson.

He was the talker and I the listener. His talk was an argument, no, *attack* against the construction of my poems. Especially *Children of Adam.*

Now, in that poem I wanted to celebrate the wonder of the human body, the male and female form. I felt it necessary to describe the parts fully. Like so-

This is the female form,
A divine nimbus exhales it from head to foot,
 it attracts with fierce undeniable attraction,
I am drawn by its breath as if I were no more than a
helpless
vapour, all falls aside but myself and it,
Books, art, religion, time, the visible and solid earth and
what was
 expected of heaven or fear'd of hell, are now consumed.

Mad filaments, ungovernable shoots play out of it,
the response likewise ungovernable,
Hair, bosom, hips, bend of legs, negligent falling hands all diffused,
mine too diffused,
Ebb stung by the flow and flow stung by the ebb, love-flesh swelling and deliciously aching,
Limitless limpid jets of love hot and enormous, quivering jelly of
love, white-blow and delirious juice,
Bridegroom night of love working surely and softly into the prostrate dawn,
Undulating into the willing and yielding day,
Lost in the cleave of the clasping and sweet-flesh'd day.

I described the female form *too* fully, Emerson seemed too think. He urged me to drop certain passages. By doing so he said I would "appeal to a larger audience, quiet the critics", and allow "all that is good about *Leaves of Grass* to shine through."
Advice ...
"What have you to say to my suggestions, Walt?" Emerson asked.

I paused. I could never hear the point better put, but I felt down in my soul the unmistakable conviction to destroy all and pursue my own way.

"Our conversation has been more precious than gold to me," I said, "but now I feel more ready than ever to adhere to my own theory and exemplify it!"

Censor? *Never!*

I want the utmost freedom, the utmost license. Censorship is always ignorant, always bad. Whether the censor is a man of virtue or a hypocrite seems to make no difference. The evil is always evil. I believe that under any responsible social order, decency will take care of itself.

I wrote 'Children of Adam' to celebrate the wonder of our human form. Was I to censor this celebration?

Oh my body! I dare not desert the likes of you in other men
 and women, nor the likes of the parts of you,
I believe the likes of you are to stand or fall with the likes of
the
 soul (and that they are the soul,)

I believe that the likes of you shall stand or fall with my
poems, and
that they are my poems,

(Anatomical slides)

Man's, woman's', child's, youth's, wife's, husband's,
mother's, father's,
young man's, young woman's, poems,
Head, neck, hair, ears, drop and tympan of the ears,
Eyes, eye fringes, iris of the eye, eyebrows and the waking
or sleeping of the lids,
Mouth, tongue, lips, teeth, roof of the mouth, jaws and the
jaw hinges,
Nose, nostrils of the nose and the partition,
Cheeks, temples, forehead, chin throat, back of the neck,
neck slue,

Strong shoulders, manly beard, scapula, hind-shoulders,
and the
ample side-round of the chest,
Upper arm, arm pit, elbow-socket, lower arm, arm sinews,
arm bones,

19

*Wrist and wrist joints, hand, palm, knuckles, thumb,
forefinger,*
finger-joints, finger-nails,
*Broad breast front, curling hair of the breast, breast-bone,
breast-side*
Rib, belly, backbone, joints of the back-bone,
*Hips, hip-sockets, hip strength, inward and outward
round, man-balls, man-root,*

Strong set of thighs well carrying the trunk above,
Leg -fibers, knee, knee-pan, upper-leg, under-leg,
Ankles, instep, foot-ball, toes, toe-joints, the heel;
*All attitudes, all the shapeliness, all the belongings of my or
your*
body or anyone's body, male or female ...

*The curious sympathy one feels when feeling with the hand
the naked meat of the body,*
The circling rivers the breath, and breathing it in and out,
*The beauty of the waist, and thence of the hips, and thence
downward toward the knees,*
*The thin red jellies within you and me, the bones and the
marrow in the bones,*

20

The exquisite realization of health;
O I say these are not the parts and poems of the body only,
but
of the soul,
O I say now these are the soul!

(Slides out.)
How people reel when I say this part or that part or bare legs and belly, Oh God! You might suppose I was citing some diabolical obscenity!

Soon after the publication of *Leaves of Grass*, I received another letter. One I do not carry with me. It was from a preacher in Maine. He said, "If I wrote more like other people and less like myself other people would like me better."
I have no doubt they would…but where would Walt Whitman come in on *that* deal?

I hear that it was charged against me that I sought to destroy institutions.
But really, I am neither for nor against institutions.

(What indeed have I in common with them? Or what with the destruction of them?)

I am not traditionally religious, I know it. But I am not anti. Yet I have been called so – irreligious, an infidel, God help me! I think the Leaves the most religious book among books, crammed full of faith! What would the *Leaves* be without faith? An empty vessel! Still, most preachers are not friendly to me. I don't despise them – it's their sermonizing and prayer that is weariness to me.

Why should I pray?
Why should I venerate and be ceremonious?
Why should I skulk or find myself indecent, while birds and animals never skulk or find themselves indecent?

I think I could turn and live with animals, they are so placid and
self contain'd.
I stand and look at them long and long.
They do not sweat and whine about their condition,
They do not lie awake in the dark and weep for their sins,

They do not make me sick discussing their duty to God,
Not one is dissatisfied, not one is demented with the mania of
owning things,
Not one kneels to another, nor to his kind that lived thousands of
years ago,
Not one is respectable or unhappy over the whole earth.

But we... we talk about salvation. We need most of all to be saved from ourselves. We need most to be saved from our own priests- priests of the churches, priests of the arts. We need that salvation in the worst way.

We have got so in our civilization that we are afraid to face the body and its issues. We shrink from the realities of our bodily life, we refer to the functions of man and woman, their sex, their passion and normal desires to something which is to be kept in the dark and lied about instead of being avowed and glorified in We will not allow it to be freely spoken of but it is still the basis of all that makes life worthwhile, don't you think?

Sex advances the horizon of discovery!

Sex, sex, sex, whether you sing, or make a machine, or go to the North Pole or love your mother or shine shoes or anything! Sex is the root of it all!

(Pause) And yet...

Even as I celebrate, I confess I am haunted by my own doubts, fears... Yes, I – Walt Whitman, a kosmos, brave, lusty, free... even I ...

Do I contradict myself?
 Very well then, I contradict myself.
 I am large. I contain multitudes.

I have made mistakes, have said things that should not have been said, have been silent when I should have spoken.

Are you the new person drawn toward me?
To begin with, take warning. I am surely far different from what you suppose;
Do you suppose yourself advancing on real ground toward a real heroic man?
 Have you no thought, O dreamer, that it may be all maya, illusion?

24

Come now, I will take you beneath this impassive exterior.
This hour I will tell things in confidence. I may not tell
  Everybody
  But I will tell you.
  There is that in me- I do not know what it is
but it is in me- it is a word unsaid.
It is not in any dictionary.

Here the frailest leaves of me and yet my strongest lasting,
here I hide and shade my thoughts.

The voices are veiled, voices unlaunch'd.

A young athlete is enamour'd of me and I of him.

But toward him there is something fierce and terrible in me
eligible to burst forth.

He masters me! Me… ever open and helpless, bereft of my
strength! Utterly abject, groveling on the ground before
him! This must *stop!*

25

*(Walt moves to desk and writes frantically. Slides of
original letter wash over Walt and entire stage)*

Stop! This cheating, childish abandonment of myself,
fancying what does not really exist in another, but is all the
time in myself alone. It is imperative, that I obviate and
remove myself from this incessant and enormous
perturbation. Give up absolutely and for good this feverish,
fluctuating, undignified pursuit! It cannot possibly be a
success! Let there be from this hour no faltering, not once,
from this hour forth for life!

(Slides out)

*(Walt stops writing, pauses) I am he that aches with
amorous love.*

*Does the earth gravitate? Does not all matter, aching,
attract all matter?*

I am he that knows the pain of unrequited love.

Agonies are one of my changes of garments.

26

(Retrieving copy of Leaves of Grass)

But now ...

I think there really is no unreturn'd love. The pay is certain one

 way or another.

 I loved a person ardently and my love was not returned.

 Yet out of that, I have written these songs.

(Reading from Leaves of Grass)

When I heard at the close of the day how my name had been

 receiv'd with plaudits in the capitol, still it was not a happy

night for me that follow'd,

And else when I carous'd, or when my plans were accomplish'd,

still I was not happy,

But the day when I rose at dawn from the bed of perfect health,

refresh'd singing, inhaling the ripe breath of autumn,

 When I saw the full moon in the west grow pale and disappear in the morning light,

When I wander'd alone over the beach, and undressing
bathed,
laughing with the cool waters, and saw the sun rise,
And when I thought how my dear friend my lover was on
his way
coming, O then I was happy,

O then each breath tasted sweeter, and all that day my food
nourish'd me more, and the beautiful day pass'd well,
And the next came with equal joy, and with the next at
evening came my friend,
And that night while all was still I heard the waters roll
slowly continually up the shores,
I heard the hissing rustle of the liquid and sands as
directed to
me whispering to congratulate me,
For the one I love most lay sleeping by me under the same
cover
in the cool night,
In the stillness, in the autumn moonbeams his face was
inclined toward me,
And his arm lay lightly around my breast - and that night I
was happy.

(Walt closes book.)
Dazzling and tremendous! How quick the sunrise would kill me,
If I could not now and always send sunrise out of me!

Writing was now my redemption- through it all, all - through the battles raging inside me and the other battles yet to come.

(A loud, persistent knocking at the door.)
No! Not now, Mrs. Davis, not yet. I'm still looking…searching… I'm not done… not finished!

(Knocking turns into drum sounds louder and louder.)

The real war, the real *Leaves of Grass*, the real Walt Whitman was yet to come.

(Drum sounds get very loud as lights fade to black.)

End Act One

30

Act Two

(In dark, drum sounds fade in, turning into knocking sounds as lights come to half.)

No! Not now, Mrs. Davis. Not yet. I'm still looking…searching…I'm not done…not finished!

(Lights to full and sound out.)

(To audience)
This is unfinished business with me…how is it with you?
I was chilled with the cold types and cylinder and wet paper between us.
I pass so poorly with paper and types…I must pass with the contact of bodies and souls.

I was simmering…searching…in many ways I hadn't even really begun.

Leaves of Grass was now in its third edition and gaining some recognition – though primarily among a small group of literati in England. In America, I was still widely unread. It had become a rallying cry with a group of men in this country – "Down Walt Whitman, down him in any way, by any method, with any weapon you can but down him, drive him into obscurity, hurry him oblivion!"

But suppose Walt Whitman stays, stays, is stubborn, stays again, will not be downed?

Afoot and lighthearted I take to the open road.
Healthy, free, brave, the world before me
The long brown path before me leading wherever I
choose…

So far so well, but the most and best of the poems, I perceived, remained unwritten. The work of my life remained to be done. The paths to the house were made, but where was the house itself?

And of those who *were* listening, I wondered, who learned my lesson complete?

Boss, journeyman, apprentice, churchman and atheist,
The stupid and the wise thinker, parents and offspring,
Merchant, clerk, porter and customer,
Editor, author, artist and schoolboy – draw nigh and
commence;

It is no lesson – it lets down the bars to a good lesson,
And that to another, and every one to another still.

It is no small matter, this round and delicious globe moving
So exactly in its orbit forever and ever, without one jolt
Or the untruth of a single second,
I do not think it was made in six days, nor in ten thousand
years, nor ten billion years,
Nor plann'd and built one thing after another as an
architect plans and builds a house.

I do not think seventy years is the time of a man or woman,
Nor that seventy million years is the time of a man or
woman,
Nor that years will ever stop the existence of me, or anyone
else.

Is it wonderful that I should be immortal? As everyone is
immortal?
I know it is wonderful, but my eyesight is equally
wonderful,
and how I was conceived in my mother's womb is equally
wonderful.
And pass'd from a babe in the creeping trance of a couple
of summers and winters to articulate and walk – all this is
equally wonderful.

And that my soul embraces you this hour, and that we affect each other is every bit as wonderful.

And that I can think such thoughts as these is just as wonderful,
And that I can remind you, and you think them and know them to be
true is just as wonderful.

And that the moon spins round the earth and on with the earth, is equally wonderful.
And that they balance themselves with the sun and stars is equally wonderful...
And I do not understand what can be more wonderful than myself!

Do I use "I" too often? *I ... I ... I?*
This isn't egotism... purely.

You see, all I have sought to do with *Leaves of Grass* is to put a person, *myself* in the latter half of the nineteenth century in America, freely, fully and truly on record.

I realized that to best express this *I* must be the center from which the poems radiate. Indeed, there could be no other. And so I was content for a long while to express this and to dote on myself.

Now, all of this might have gone on and on and come to naught had I not been shaken – blasted out of my self-absorption – by the occurrence of our Civil War.

(A cannon blast)
It was the war – it's sights and sounds and the thousands – the tens and twenties of thousands of American young men wounded, operated on, dying, that opened a new world to me somehow... made me explore deeper mines than any yet. It was the war that really made me pray, brought me to my real knees.

The year was 1861.
Year that trembled and reeled beneath me!
Your summer wind was warm enough,
Yet the air I breathed froze me.
A thick gloom fell thru the sunshine
And darkened me.

I cried out-

Must I change my triumphant songs?
Must I indeed learn to chant the cold dirges
Of the baffled and sullen hymns of defeat?
There could be no dainty rhymes or sentimental love verses for you, terrible year. I wrote a rally cry!

(Drums)
Beat! Beat! Drums! – Blow! Bugles! Blow!
Through the windows – through the doors – burst like a ruthless force,
Into the solemn church, and scatter the congregation,
Into the school where the scholar is studying;
Leave not the bridegroom quiet – no happiness must he have now with his bride,
nor the peaceful farmer any peace, ploughing his field or gathering his grain,
so fierce you whir and pound you drums – so shrill you bugles blow.
The day was April 12, I remember clearly. I had just left the opera and was walking down Broadway to the Brooklyn ferry.

Suddenly, I heard the cries of the newspaper boys who came tearing and yelling up the street. There had been a firing on Fort Sumpter and the United States flag in Charlestown. This marked the start of the succession war.

Beat! Beat! Drums! – Blow! Bugles! Blow!
Over the traffic of cities – over the rumble of wheels in the streets;
Are beds prepared for sleepers at night in the houses? No sleepers
must sleep in those beds,
Would the talkers be talking? Would the singer attempt to sing? ...
Then rattle quicker, heavier drums – you bugles wilder blow!

The crowd read the headlines, shivering in small groups in the rain. I can see them there now under the lamps at midnight. I can see their faces again.

You know, I don't think the war seemed so horrible to me at the time, when I was busy in the midst of its barbarism as it does now in retrospect.

Still, I never once questioned the decision that led me into the war and to Washington- whatever the years have brought, whatever sickness, whatnot- I have accepted the results as inevitable and right.

I entered the war to find my brother George.

George was quick to enlist with the thirteenth regiment. You see, in New York and Brooklyn, we all thought the rebellion would be crushed in a few days or weeks but, oh, this feeling was quickly reversed by battle after battle... and then the shock...my family received news that George had been wounded- dead for all we knew.

I quickly left for Washington to find him.

(At desk, sorting)
Letters.
My memories of war are filled with letters. Letters piled high, letters strewn. Some cherished, some never opened. Letters to lovers. Letters from mothers to son's and from son's to mothers.

This was my first-
(Slide of Mrs. Whitman)
Dear, Dear Mother,

I succeeded in reaching the camp of the 51st, N.Y. and found George alive and well. When I found out this was so you may imagine how trifling all my little cares and difficulties seemed – they vanished into nothing- and now that I have lived for eight or nine days amid such scenes as the camps furnish, and had a practiced part in it all, and realized the way hundreds of thousands of good men are now living – not only without comforts but with death and sickness – really nothing we call trouble is worth talking about. One of the first things that met my eyes in camp was a heap of feet, arms, and legs under a tree in front of the hospital…

George was wounded by a shell, a gash in the cheek but it has healed without difficulty already.

I will stay here for the present – long enough to see if I can get any employment. Of course, I am unsettled at the moment.

Dear Mother, my love,

Walt

(Slide out.)

I stayed.

I stayed throughout most of the war. I worked as a government clerk and wrote essays for the New York papers. But my real work was visiting the sick and wounded in the hospitals. In a sense this was the most real work of my life. Books are all very well but this sort of thing is so much better...don't you think? As life in life is always superior to life in a book.

For four years I saw war where war is worst. Not on the battlefields, no, in the hospitals. There war is worst. I mixed with it.

(Slide of Civil War hospital ward.)
(Walt puts on coat, hat and prepares himself for his visiting ritual. Moving into hospital area he kneels at several bedsides)

My habit was to prepare for my daily and nightly visits, which lasted for four or five hours each, by fortifying myself with a good night's rest, a bath, clean clothes, a good meal and – this is important – as cheerful a presence as possible.

The soldiers are mere lads, many only seventeen years old. As I pass from boy to boy I try to give a word or a trifle without exception. I give all kinds of sustenance: blackberries, lemons and sugar, wine, brandy and tobacco, handkerchiefs. I always give paper, envelopes and stamps. Then I select the most needy cases and devote my time and services to them.

To many of these young men there is something in personal love, caresses and the magnetic flood of sympathy and friendship that does, in its way, more good than all the medicine in the world …

So I go round.

Some of my boys get well, some of my boys die.

(Slide out)

(Back to desk)

Letters.

Another to be written, another to be read.

(Slide of soldier)

Mr. and Mrs. Haskell,

Dear friends, I thought it would be soothing to you to have a few words about the last days of your son Erastus Haskell of Company K. I write in haste, and nothing of importance only I thought anything about Erastus would be welcome.

From the time he came to Armory Square Hospital till he died, there was hardly a day but I was with him a portion of the time.

I had no opportunity to do much, or anything for him, as nothing was needed, only to wait the progress of his malady. I am only a friend visiting the wounded and sick soldiers, (not connected with any society or State.) From the first I felt that Erastus was in danger, or at least was much worse than they in the hospital supposed.

I was very anxious he should be saved, and so were they all. He was well used by the attendants – poor boy, I can see him as I write – he was tanned and had a fine head of hair, and looked good in the face when he first came, and was in pretty good flesh too – (he had his hair cut close about ten or twelve days before he died) - he never complained – but it looked pitiful to see him lying there, with such a look out of his eyes. He had large clear eyes, they seemed to talk. Many nights I sat in the hospital by his bedside till far in the night – the lights would be put out – yet I would sit there silently, hours, late, perhaps fanning him – he always liked to have me sit there, but never cared to talk – I shall never forget those nights, it was a curious and solemn scene, the sick and wounded lying around in their cots, just visible in the darkness, and this dear young man close at hand lying on what proved to be his death bed. I do not know his past life, but what I saw of him, he was a noble boy – I felt he was one I should get very much attached to.

Poor dear boy, though you were not my son, I felt to love you as a son, what short time I saw you sick and dying there. But it is well as it is – perhaps better. Who knows whether he is not far better off, that patient and sweet young soul, to go, than we are to stay? Farewell, dear boy. You did not lay there among strangers without having one near who loved you dearly, and to whom you gave your dying kiss.

Mr. and Mrs. Haskell, I think you have reason to be proud of such a son, and all his relatives have causes to treasure his memory. I write to you this letter because I would do something at least in his memory; his fate was a hard one, to die so. He is one of the thousands of our unknown American young men in the ranks about whom there is no record or fame, no fuss made about their dying so unknown, but I find in them the real precious and loyal ones of this land, giving themselves up – aye, even their young and precious lives, in their country's cause.

Though we are strangers and shall probably never see each other, I send you and all Erastus' brothers and sisters my love.

Walt Whitman

(Slide out)

Have you seen someone die?
Have you had the privilege?
I have.

Hundreds of times.

I have witnessed the deaths of these brave young men.

I have leaned close and whispered to them. I have kissed their lips and wished them well on their way. Vigils wondrous… strange…beautiful.

What indeed is finally beautiful except death and love?

(Walt moves to sit on ground aside dead soldier.)

Vigil strange I kept on the field one night;
When you my son and my comrade dropped at my side that day,
One look I but gave which your dear eyes return'd with look I
shall never forget,
One touch of your hand to mine O boy, reach'd up as you lay
on the ground,
Then onward I sped in the battle, the even – contested battle,
Til late in the night reliev'd to the place at last again I made my way,

Found you in death so cold dear comrade, found your body
son of responding kisses,
(never again on earth responding,)
Bared your face in the starlight, curious the scene, cool
Blew the moderate night-wind,
Long there and then in vigil I stood, dimly around me the
battle field spreading,
Vigil wondrous and vigil sweet there in the fragrant silent
night,
But not a tear fell, not even a long-drawn sigh, long, long,
I gazed,

Then on the earth partially reclining sat by your side
Leaning my chin in my hands,
Passing sweet hours, immortal and mystic hours with you
Dearest comrade – not a tear, not a word,
Vigil of silence, love and death, vigil for you my son and my
soldier,

As onward silently stars aloft, eastward new ones upward
stole, vigil final for you brave boy, (I could not save you
swift was your death, I faithfully loved you and cared for
you living, I think we shall surely meet again,)

*Till at latest lingering of the night, indeed just as the dawn
appear'd my comrade I wrapt in his blanket, enveloped
well his form,*

*Folded the blanket well, tucking it carefully over head and
Carefully under feet,
And there and then and bathed by the rising sun, my son in
His grave, in his rude – dug grave I deposited,
Ending my vigil strange with that, vigil of night and
Battlefield dim,
Vigil for boy of responding kisses, (never again on earth
responding,)
Vigil for comrade swiftly slain, vigil I never forget, how as
day brightened,
I rose from the chill ground and folded my soldier well in
his blanket,
And buried him where he fell.*

*(Walt rises, takes boutonniere from his coat lapel and
places it at the foot of dead soldier. He slowly dons hat,
retrieves cane and returns to Walt Whitman at seventy.)*

Such was the war.

It was not a quadrille in a ballroom. Future years will never know the seething hell and countless scenes- and it is best they should not. The real war will never get in the books. Its interior history will not only not be written, the deeds and passions will never even be suggested. And the actual soldier, with all his ways – his incredible dauntlessness, tastes and language – his fierce friendship, strength and animality I say will never be written.

And perhaps should not be.

So goodbye to war.

And now I say goddam'em...goddam'em, goddam'em, goddam'em! All wars! The whole business is about nine hundred and ninety-nine parts diarrhea to one part glory. All the loss, the pain...

Well...such things are gloomy...

Yet even these things have their place. There is a saying, "God doeth all things well," the meaning of which, after due time has appeared to my soul.

No array of terms can say how much I am now at peace about God
and about death.
I hear and behold God in every object, yet understand God not in the least.

Why should I wish to see God better than this day?
I see something of God each hour of the twenty-four and each moment then,
And in the faces of men and women I see God
And in my own face in the glass.

As to you, death, and you bitter hug of mortality,
It is idle to try to alarm me.

I am the poet of death as well as the poet of life.
I welcome you.

Come lovely and soothing death,
Undulate around the world, serenely arriving,
Arriving, in the day, in the night, to all,
To each, sooner or later delicate death.
And as to you, corpse, I think you are good manure, but
that does not offend me.
I smell the white roses, sweet scented and growing,
I reach to the leafy lips, I reach
To the polished breasts of melons.
As to you, life, I reckon you are the leavings of many
deaths.
No doubt I have died myself ten thousand times before.

What do you think has become of the young and old men?
And what do you think has become of the women and
children?

They are alive and well somewhere,
The smallest sprout shows there is really no death,
And if ever there was it led forward life, and does not wait
at the end to arrest it,
and ceas'd the moment life appear'd.

All goes onward and outward, nothing collapses,
And to die is different from what any one supposed,
 and luckier.

Do you see? It is not chaos or death. It is form, union, plan. It is eternal life. It is happiness.

Just happiness.

(Walt retrieves copy of Leaves of Grass)

We must work, you see, at finding beauty in this life, work at being grateful.

Yes. *I am grateful.*

I am grateful for your visit. Looking back with you has made me realize a man has never really been more fortunate than I have been in having things done just as he demands them. Take *Leaves of Grass* for instance.

It certainly is what I, I alone designed it should be.

Proud. Proud indeed we may be, my book and I! Why should I call it a failure? Why? Why this endless questioning of myself? Whether lost, lost at last, unaccepted, unread – there at least it is – direct from my hands.

O me! O life! Of the questions of these recurring,
Of the endless trains of the faithless, of cities fill'd with the foolish,
Of myself forever reproaching myself, (for who more foolish than I, and who more faithless?)
Of eyes that vainly crave the light, of the objects mean, of the struggle ever renew'd,
Of the poor results of all, of the plodding and sordid crowds I see around me,
Of the empty and useless years of the rest, with the rest me intertwined,
The question, O me! So sad, recurring---What good amid these, O me, O life?
Answer: That you are here—that life exists and identity,
That the powerful play goes on, and you may contribute a verse.

This is what you shall do …

Love the earth and sun and the animals, despise riches, give alms to everyone that asks, stand up for the stupid and crazy, devote your labor and income to others, hate tyrants, argue not concerning God, have patience and indulgence toward the people, take off your hat to nothing known or unknown or to any man or number of men, go freely with powerful uneducated persons and with the young and with the mothers of families, read these leaves in the open air every season of every year of your life, re-examine all you have been told at school or church or in any book, dismiss whatever insults your own soul, and your very flesh shall be a great poem and have the richest fluency not only in its words but in the silent lines of its lips and face and between the lashes of your eyes and in every motion and joint of your body-

(Walt discovers Horace's notebook.)

Is that …? *It is!* I've *found* it! Horace's notebook! Oh, he'll be glad to have this back. This collection of ramblings of an old, grey poet.

I *have* developed a knack for gabbing and
loitering…perhaps you've noticed.
I've even taken to talking to myself at times,
especially while walking in the woods.

The spotted hawk swoops by and accuses me, he complains
of my gab and loitering.
I too am not a bit tamed, I too am untranslatable,
I sound my barbaric yawp over the roofs of the world.

(A knock at the door) Yes, Mrs. Davis? *(Listens)* On its
way? So soon?

(To audience) Horace and the carriage are coming. I'll have
to say so long!

I've enjoyed our visit – no, more than that, it fortified me. I
feel ready to celebrate my seventieth birthday after all! A
glass of champagne won't kill me. Indeed, if I had my way
I'd crack a bottle every day. It does me no harm.

So long!

I depart as air, I shake my locks at the runaway sun,
I effuse my flesh in eddies, and drift it in lacey jags.

I bequeath myself to the dirt to grow from the grass I love,
If you want me again, look for me under your boot-soles.

You will hardly know who I am or what I mean,
But I shall be good health to you nevertheless,
And filter and fibre your blood.
Failing to fetch me at first keep encouraged,
Missing me one place search another,
I stop somewhere waiting for you

(The sounds of a carriage approaching. Lights start to fade.)

(Walt at window) Horace! I've *found* it! I'm here! I'm ready! Horace!

End of Play

Made in the USA
Middletown, DE
07 March 2015